18 Current and Classic Hits

Arranged by Dan Coates

Simply Country is a collection of classic and contemporary songs by some of the greatest country music artists. These songs have been carefully selected and arranged by Dan Coates for Easy Piano, making them accessible to pianists of all ages. Phrase markings, articulations, fingering and dynamics have been included to aid with interpretation, and a large print size makes the notation easy to read.

This collection represents superstars from country music's past and present: Hank Williams, John Denver, Garth Brooks, Tammy Wynette, Faith Hill, Clint Black, Carrie Underwood, and many others. Their songs range from Alan Jackson's honky tonk toe-tapper "Don't Rock the Jukebox" to Hank Williams' bittersweet "Your Cheatin' Heart" to Tim McGraw's inspiring "Live Like You Were Dying." Each melody, whether upbeat and snappy or slow and lyrical, is a pleasure to both sing and play. With its spirit and charm, this music has been embraced by musicians and audiences, young and old, around the world. For these reasons and more, country music is exciting to explore.

After all, it is *Simply Country*!

Cover illustration by Sarah Lewis

Contents

Annie's Song

Words and Music by John Denver
Arranged by Dan Coates

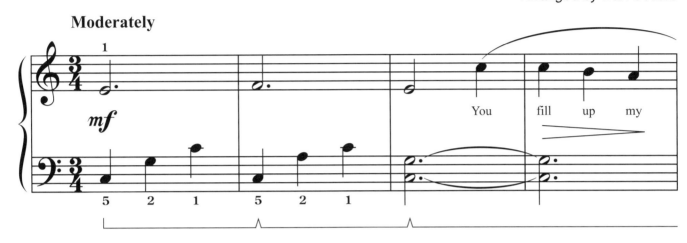

4

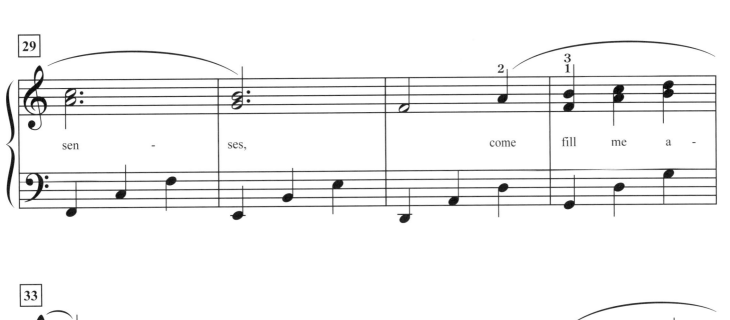

29

sen - ses,   come fill me a -

33

gain.   Come let me

37

love   you,   let me give my life
sen - ses   like a night in the

mf

41

to you,_____   let me drown in your
for - est,_____   like the moun - tains in

6

love you,
sen - ses,

come love me a -
come fill me a -

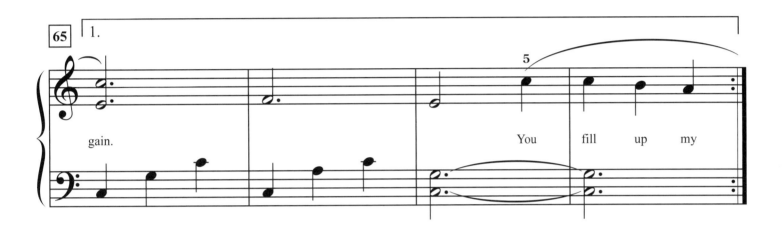

1.

gain.

You fill up my

2.

gain.

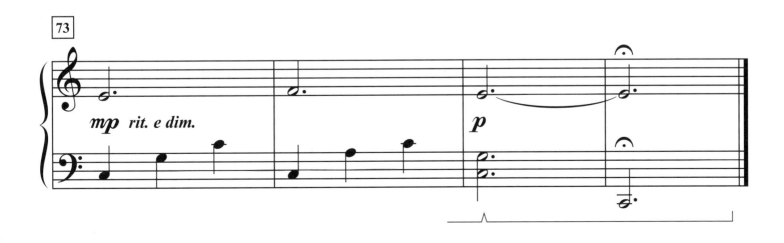

mp *rit. e dim.*

p

The Dance

Words and Music by Tony Arata
Arranged by Dan Coates

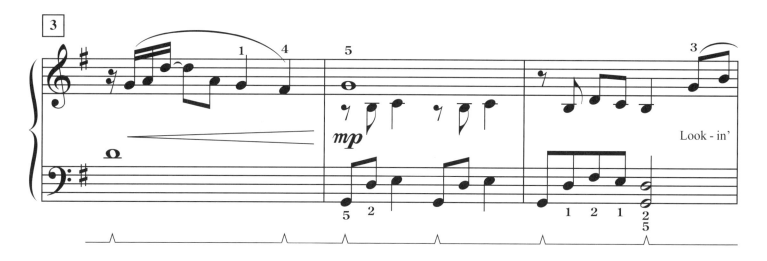

Look - in'

back on the mem - 'ry of the
you, I held ev - 'ry - thing. For a

Desperado

Words and Music by
Don Henley and Glenn Frey
Arranged by Dan Coates

Des - per - a - do,   why don't you
            - a - do,   oh, you ain't

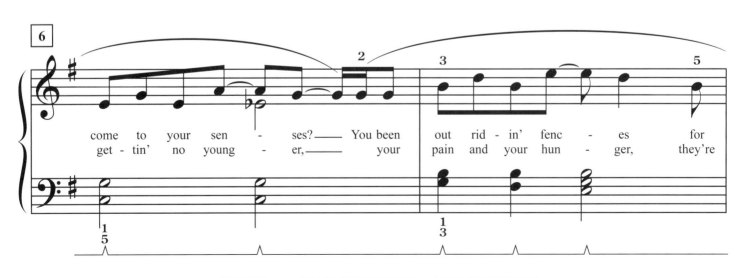

come to your sen - ses? _____ You been   out rid - in' fenc - es   for
get - tin' no young - er, _____ your   pain and your hun - ger,   they're

Don't It Make My Brown Eyes Blue

Words and Music by Richard Leigh
Arranged by Dan Coates

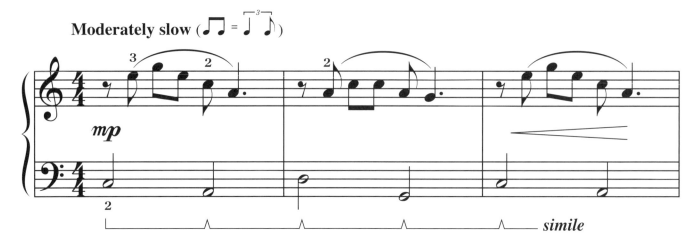

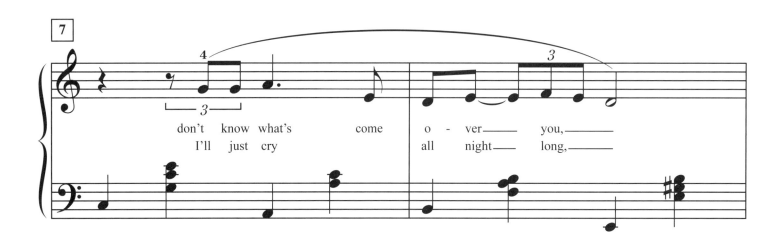

you've found some-one new _____ and don't it make my brown eyes
say it is - n't true _____ and

blue. _____

don't it make my brown eyes blue.

mf Tell me no se - crets, tell me some lies, give me no rea - sons, — give me

al - i - bis. Tell me you love me and don't____ let me cry,

say____ an-y-thing but don't say good-bye. I did-n't mean____

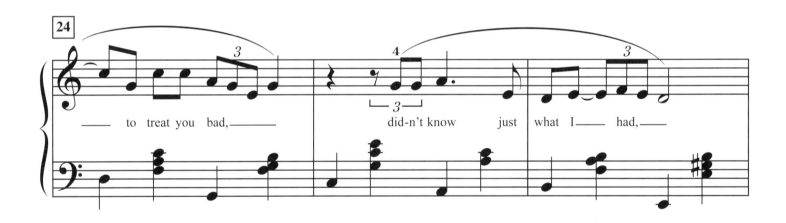

____ to treat you bad,____ did-n't know just what I____ had,____

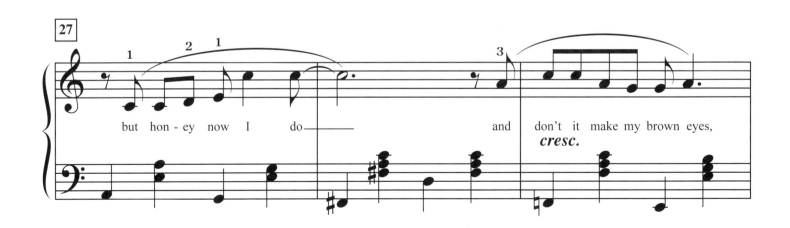

but hon-ey now I do____ and don't it make my brown eyes,

don't it make my brown eyes, don't it make my brown eyes blue.

mf

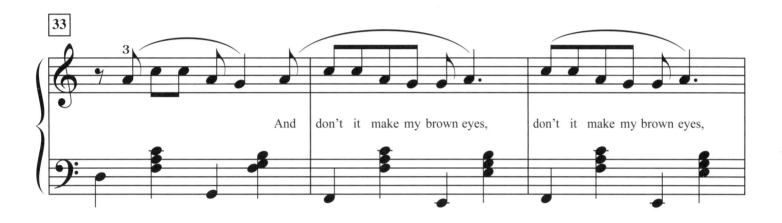

And don't it make my brown eyes, don't it make my brown eyes,

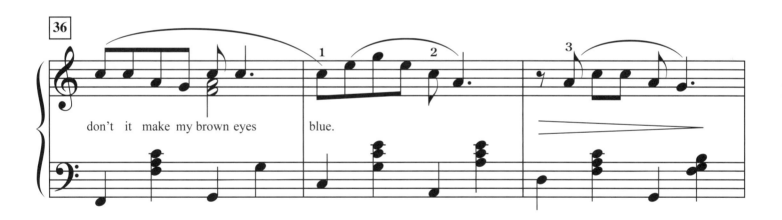

don't it make my brown eyes blue.

mp *rit. e dim.* *p*

Don't Rock the Jukebox

Words and Music by Alan Jackson,
Roger Murrah and Keith Stegall
Arranged by Dan Coates

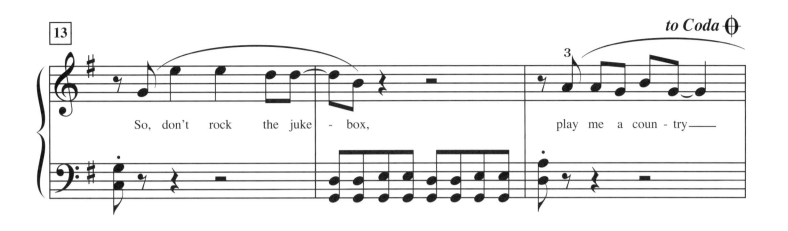

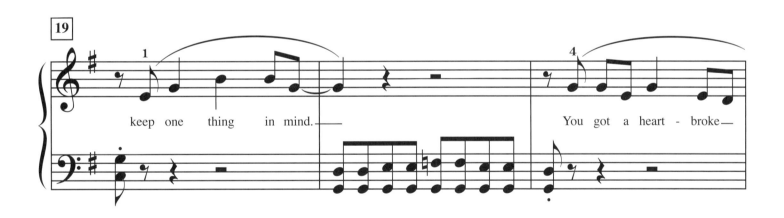

How Do I Live

Words and Music by Diane Warren
Arranged by Dan Coates

you ev - er leave,___ ba - by, you would take a - way ev - 'ry - thing.

Need you with me.___ Ba - by, 'cause you know that you're ev - 'ry - thing

good in my life.___ And tell me

now, how do I live with - out___ you? I want to know.

I Cross My Heart

Words and Music by
Steve Dorff and Eric Kaz
Arranged by Dan Coates

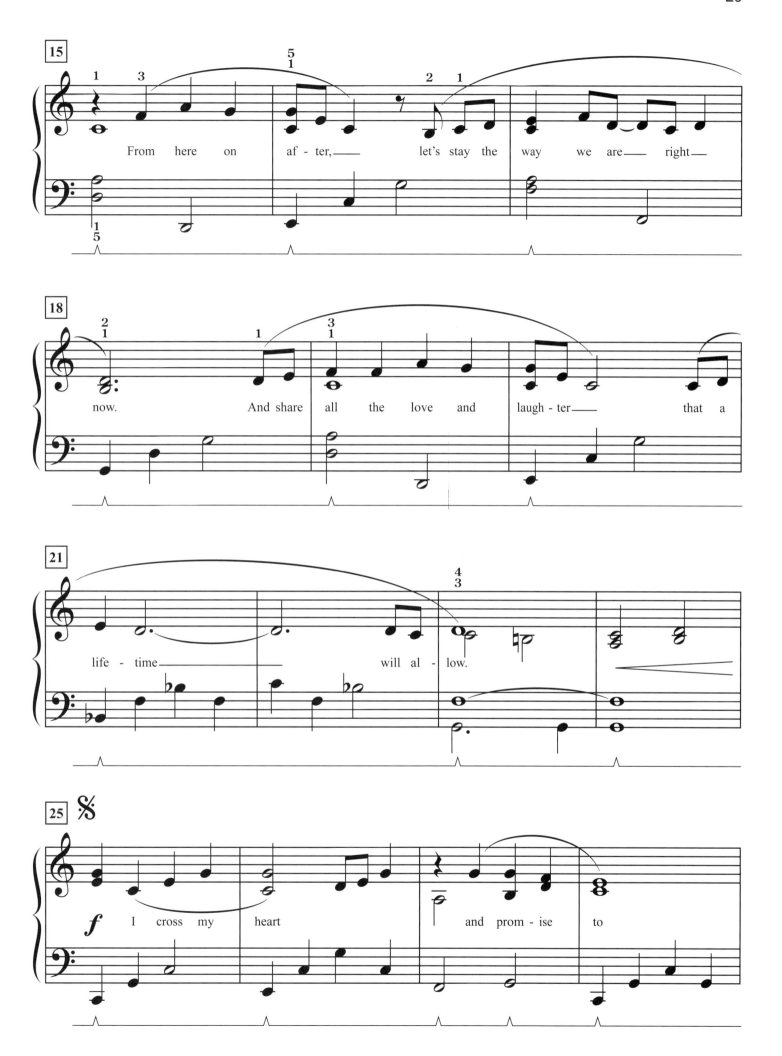

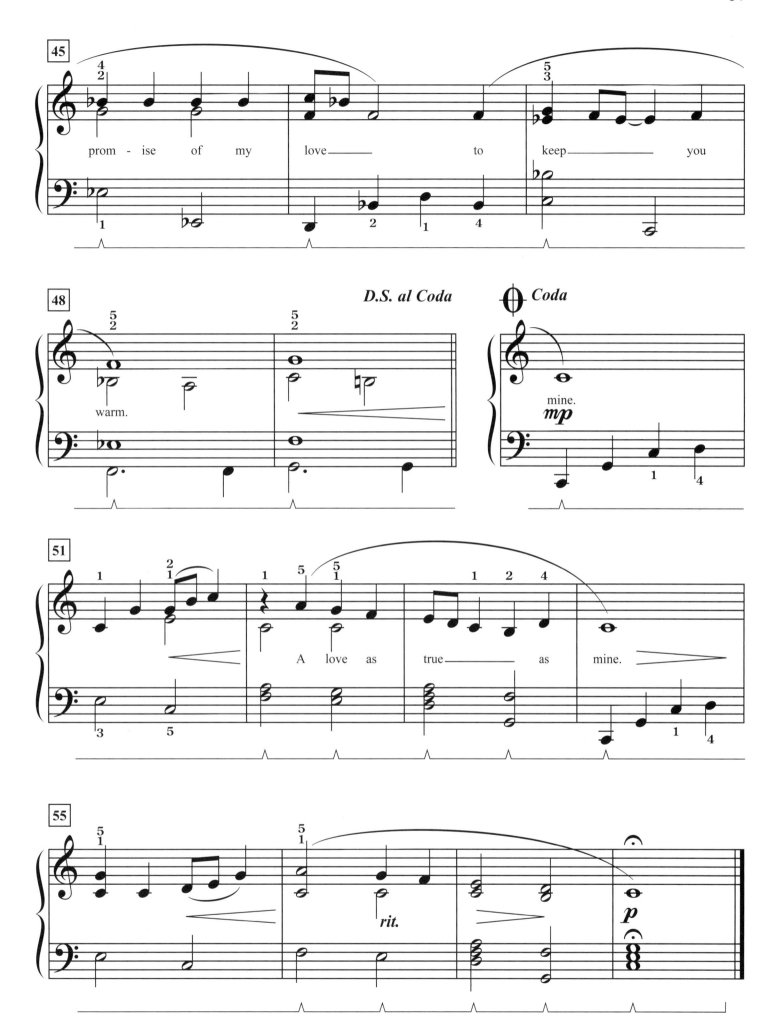

I Swear

Words and Music by
Gary Baker and Frank Myers
Arranged by Dan Coates

Moderately slow

I see the ques - tion in ___ your eyes,
I'll give you ev - 'ry - thing ___ I can,

34

Inside Your Heaven

Words and Music by Andreas Carlsson,
Per Nylen and Savan Kotecha
Arranged by Dan Coates

Live Like You Were Dying

Words and Music by
Tim Nichols and Craig Wiseman
Arranged by Dan Coates

Moderately slow

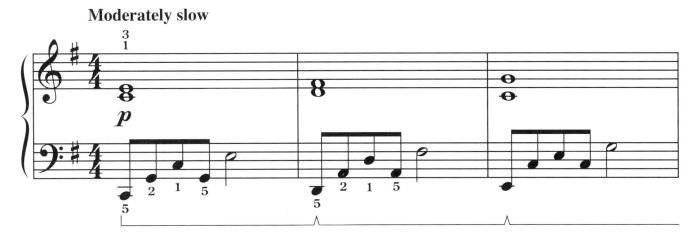

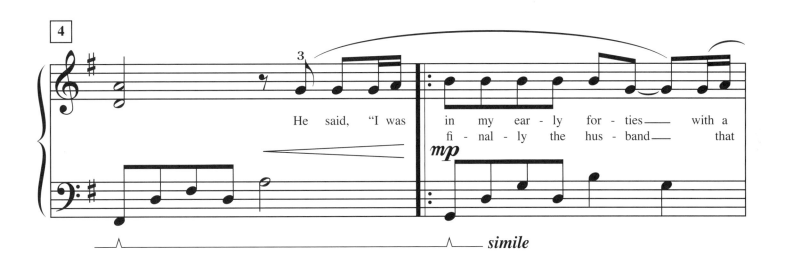

He said, "I was in my ear - ly for - ties—— with a
fi - nal - ly the hus - band—— that

lot of life be - fore me,—— when a
most the time I was - n't, and I be -

mo - ment came that stopped me on a
came a friend a friend would like to

42

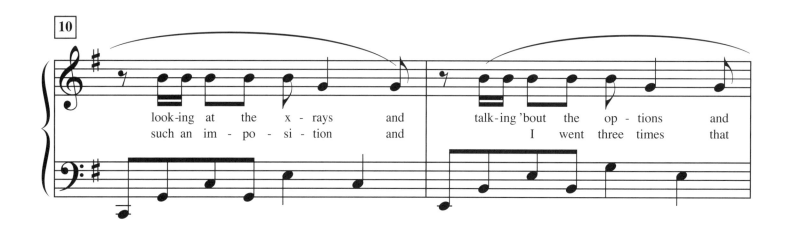

ny - ing." And he said, "Some - day I hope you get the

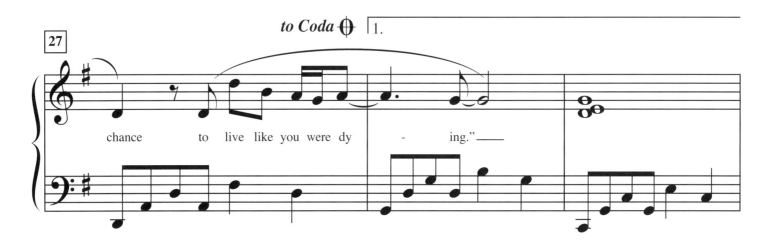

to Coda ⊕ 1.

chance to live like you were dy - ing."——

2.

He said, "I was - ing. Like to -

mor - row was a gift and you've got e - ter - ni - ty to think a - bout what'd you

mp

do with it.   And what did you   do with it?"   What did I

cresc.

D.S. al Coda

do with it?   What would I   do with it?   "I went

Coda

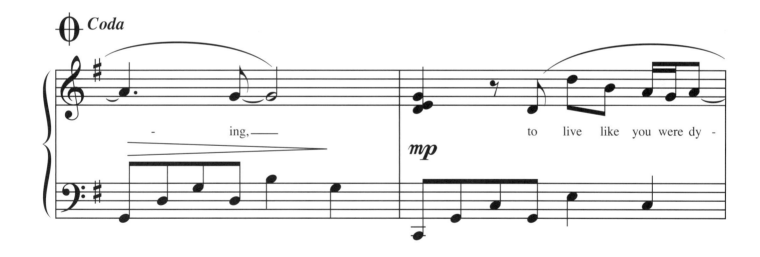

- ing,_____   to live like you were dy -

mp

ing."_____   *rit. e dim.*

p

Lane's Theme

Composed by Bill Conti
Arranged by Dan Coates

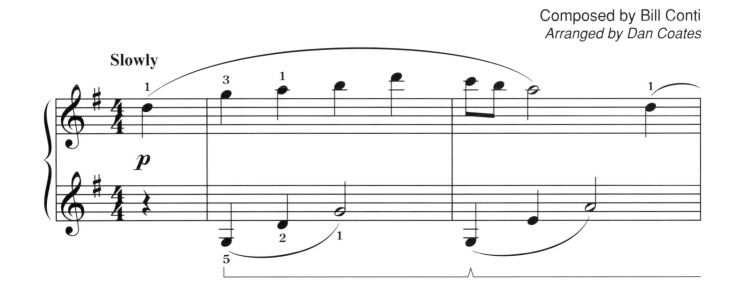

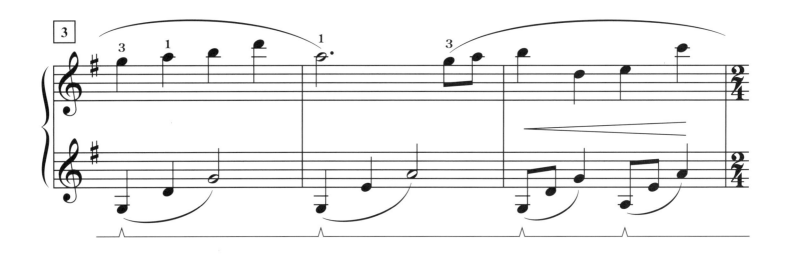

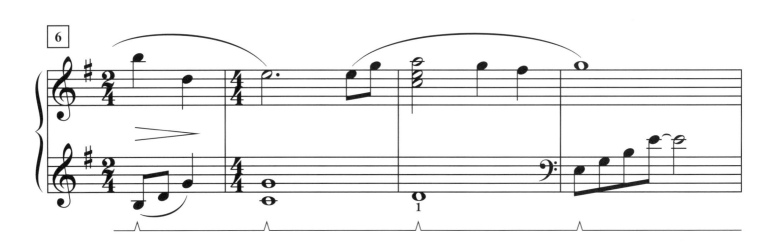

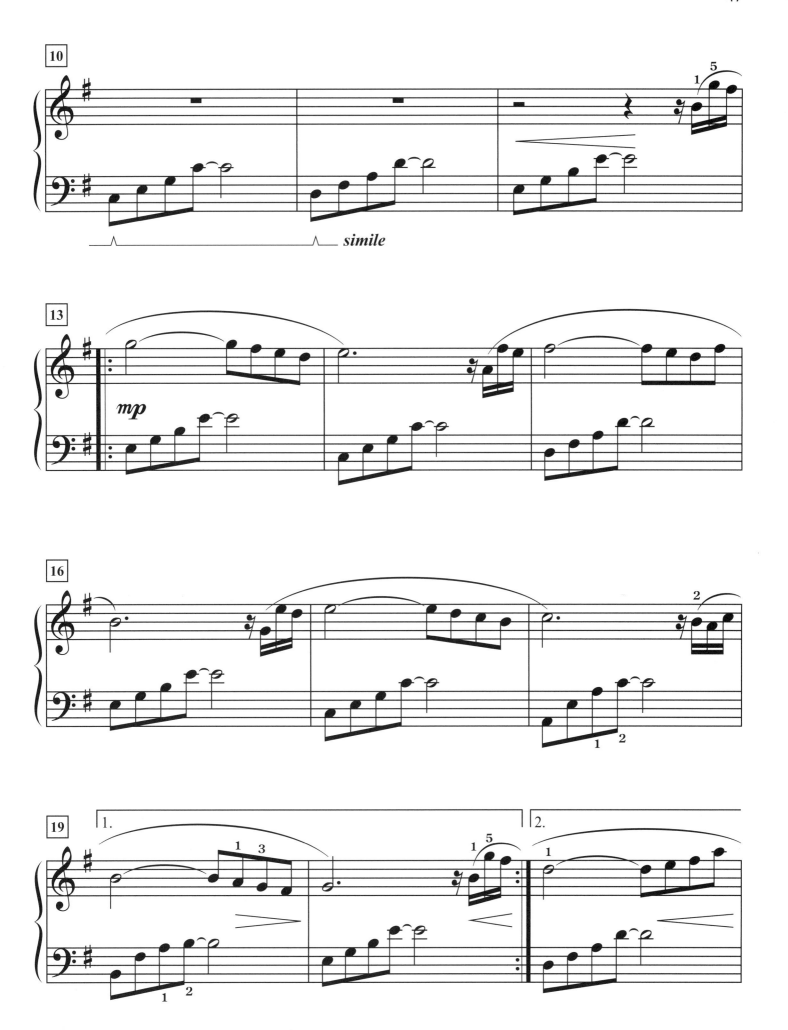

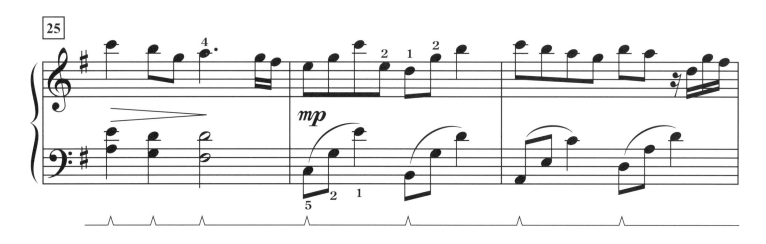

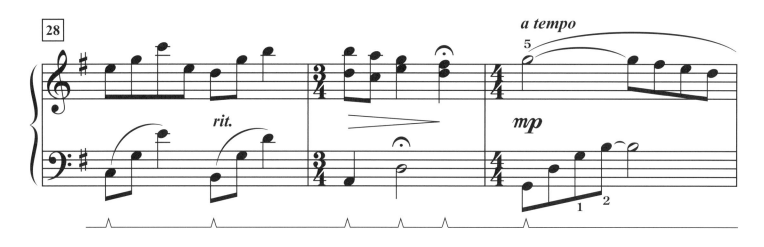

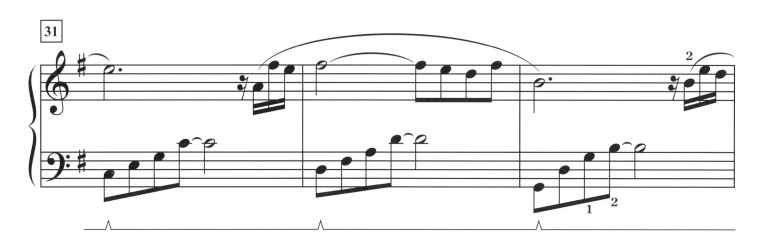

Let Me Let Go

Words and Music by
Dennis Morgan and Steve Diamond
Arranged by Dan Coates

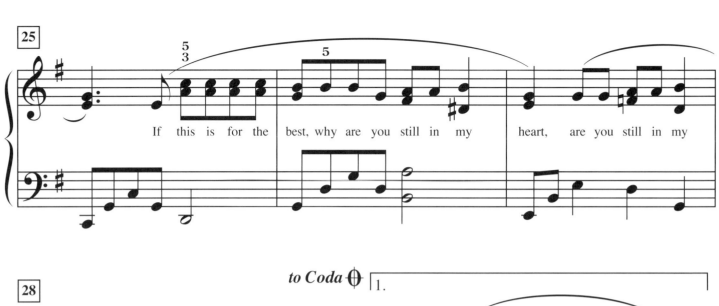
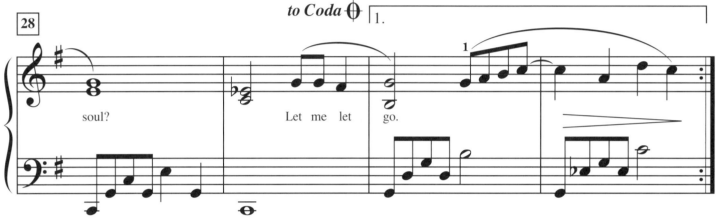
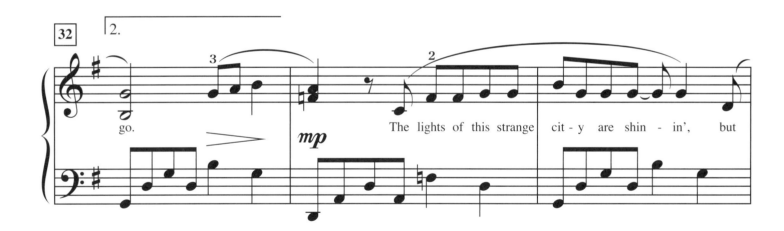

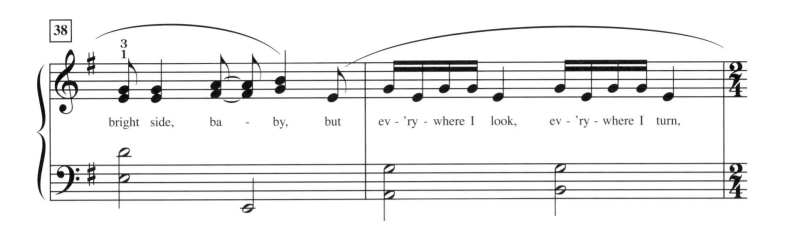

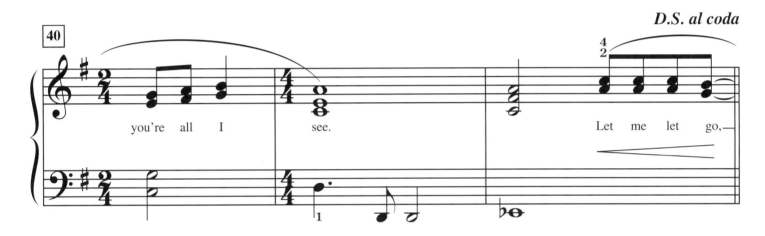

Somebody Like You

Words and Music by
John Shanks and Keith Urban
Arranged by Dan Coates

There's a new wind blow - in' like I've
run in cir - cles, go - in'

nev - er known.___ I'm breath - in' deep - er than I've
no - where fast.___ I'd take one step for - ward, end up

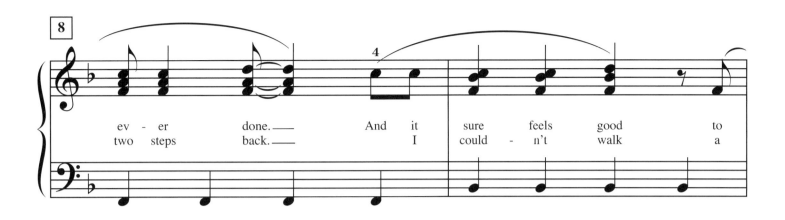

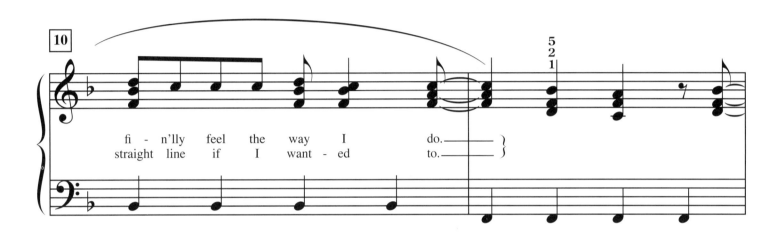

shin - ing down on me and you.

When you put your arms a - round me, you

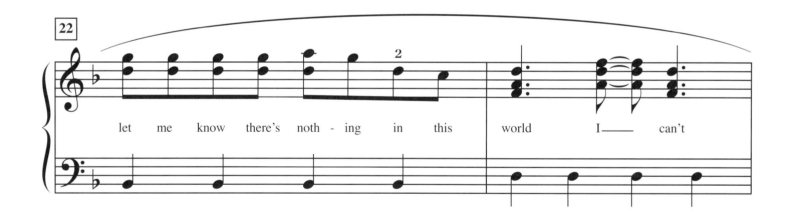

let me know there's noth - ing in this world I can't

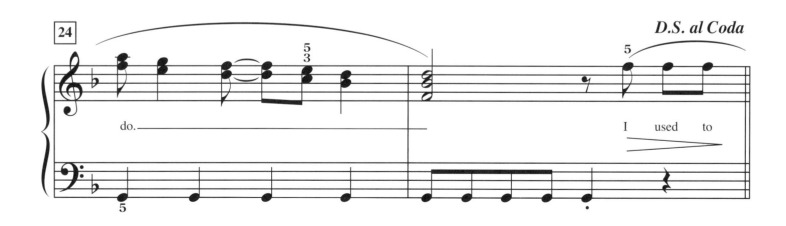

D.S. al Coda

do. I used to

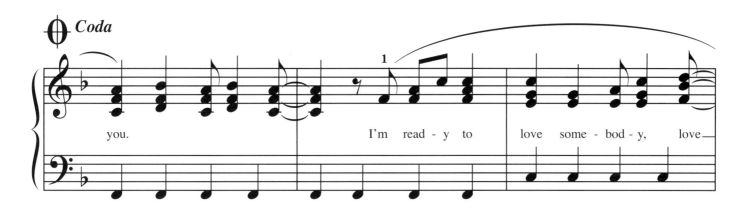

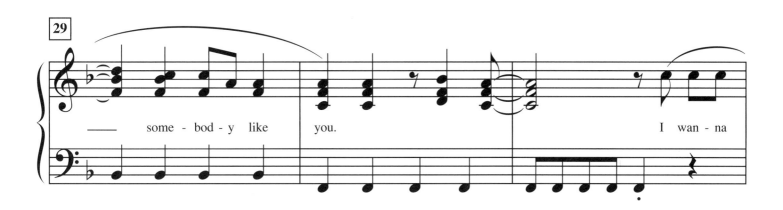

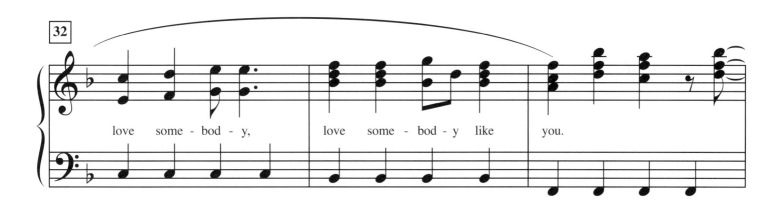

Something That We Do

Words and Music by
Clint Black and Skip Ewing
Arranged by Dan Coates

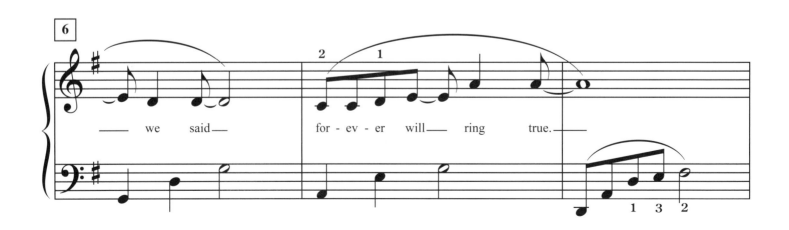

Your Cheatin' Heart

Words and Music by Hank Williams
Arranged by Dan Coates

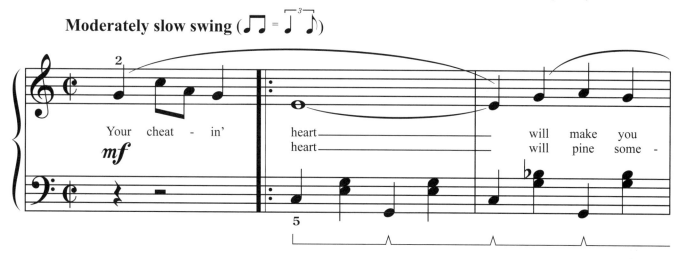

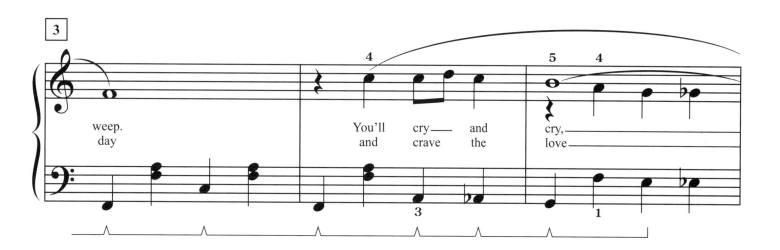

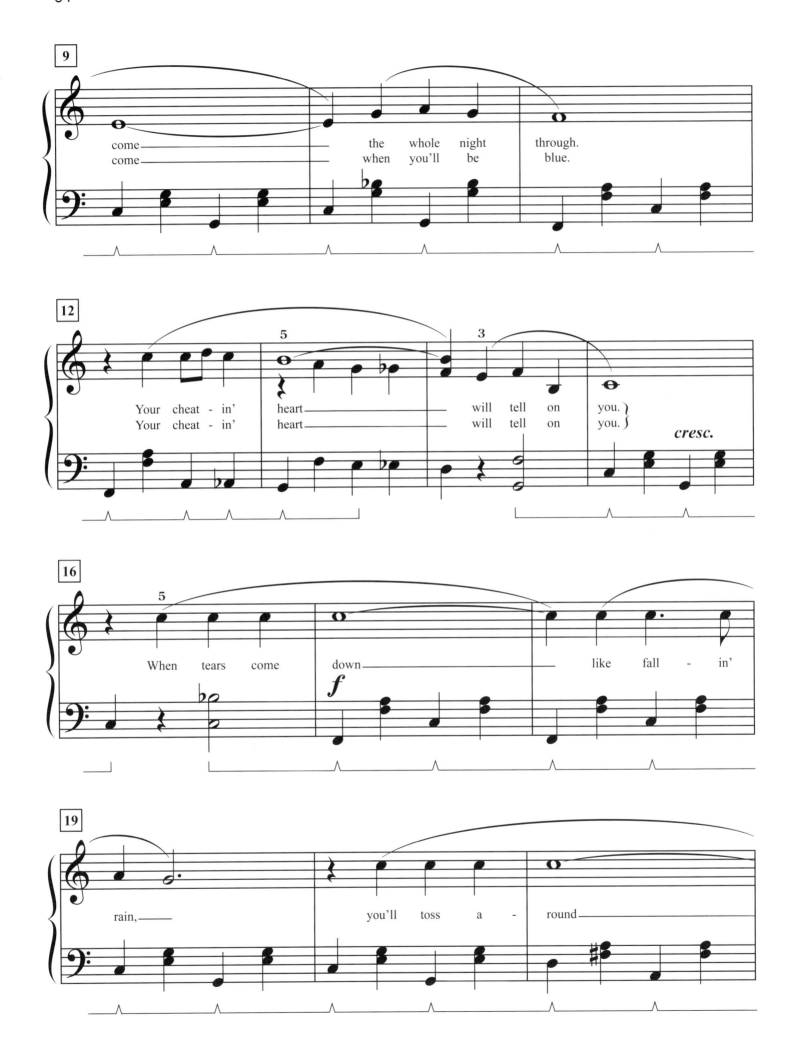

Stand by Your Man

Words and Music by
Tammy Wynette and Billy Sherill
Arranged by Dan Coates

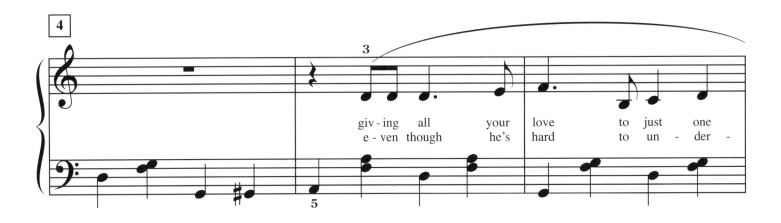

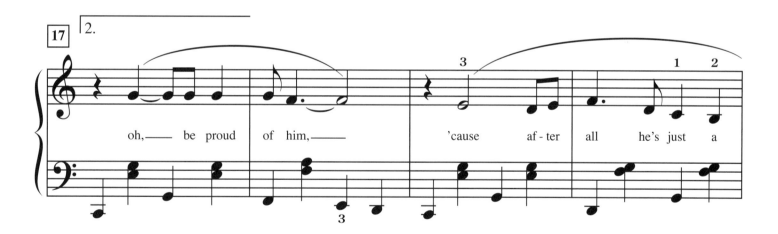

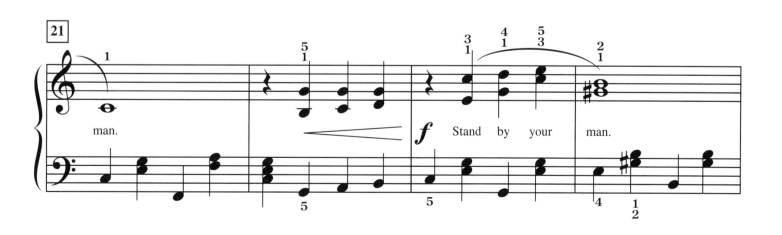

68

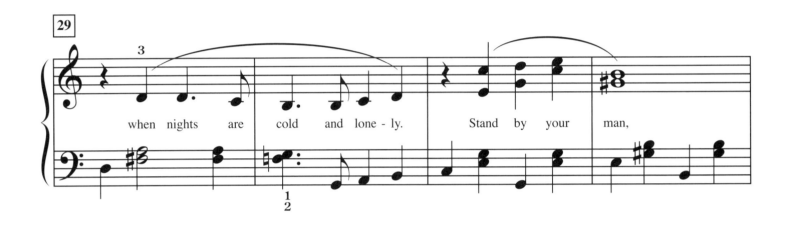

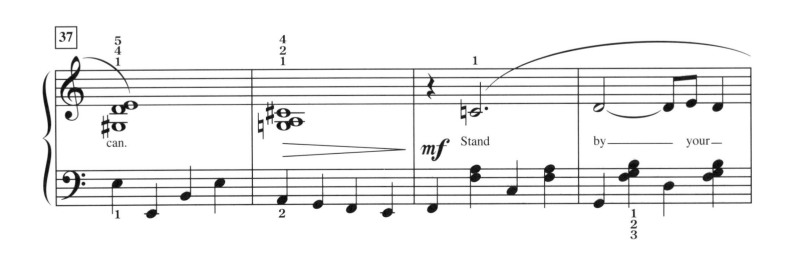

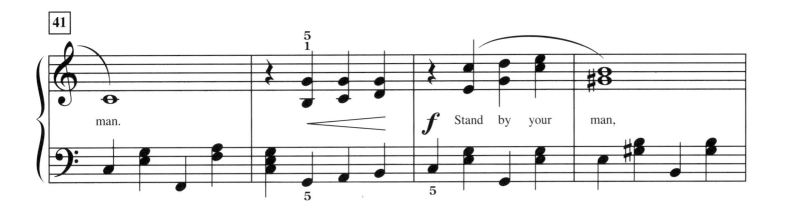

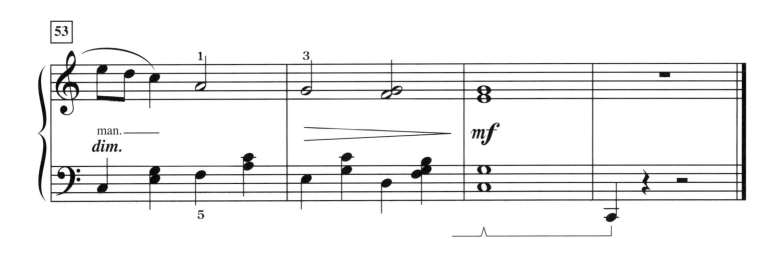

Sunshine on My Shoulders

Words by John Denver
Music by John Denver, Mike Taylor and Dick Kniss
Arranged by Dan Coates

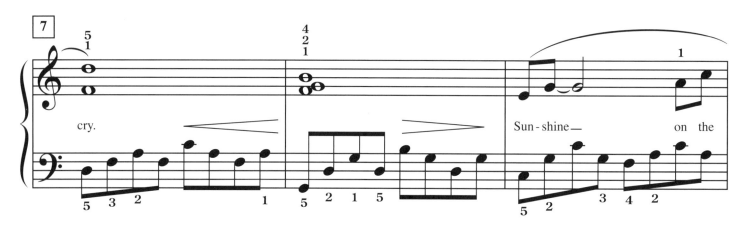

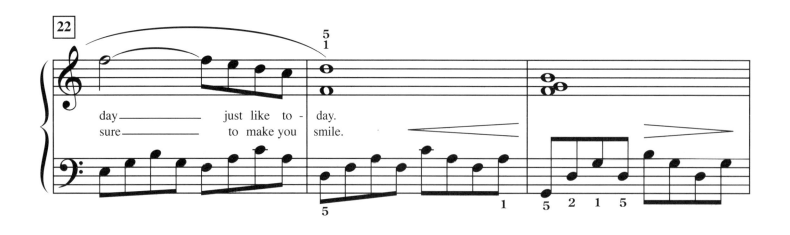

day————————— just like to - day.
sure————————— to make you smile.

If I——— had a song that I could sing for you,—
If I——— had a wish that I could wish for you,—

I'd sing a song——— to make you feel this
I'd make a wish——— for sun - shine all the

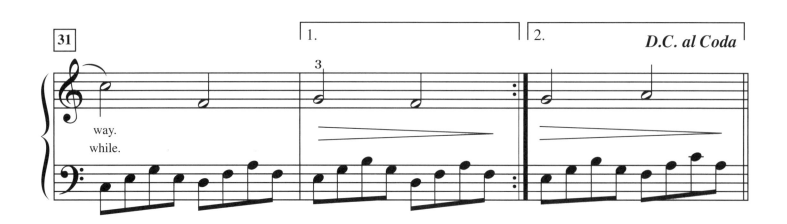

way.
while.

Sun-shine— al-most all the time makes me high.———

Sun-shine— al-most al-ways...———

dim. poco a poco

This Kiss

Words and Music by Robin Lerner,
Annie Roboff and Beth Nielsen Chapman
Arranged by Dan Coates

Moderately bright, in 2

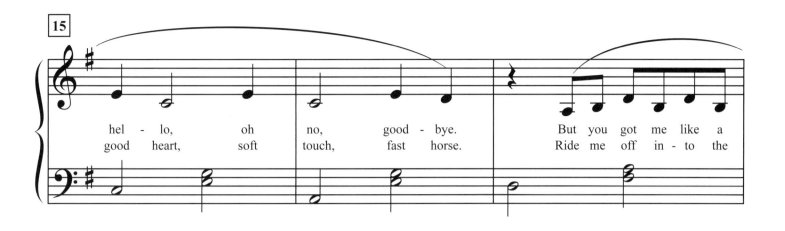

hel - lo, oh no, good - bye. But you got me like a
good heart, oh soft touch, fast horse. Ride me off in - to the

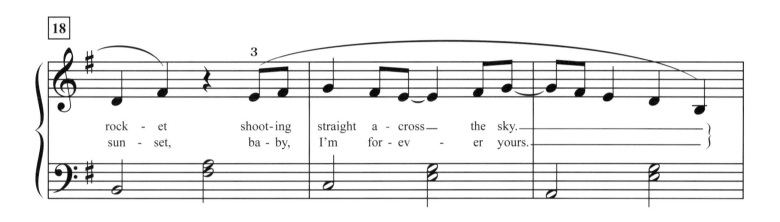

rock - et shoot-ing straight a - cross the sky.
sun - set, ba - by, I'm for - ev - er yours.

It's the way you love me. It's a feel-ing like this.

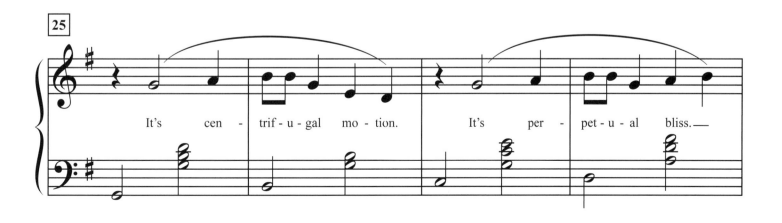

It's cen - trif - u - gal mo - tion. It's per - pet - u - al bliss.

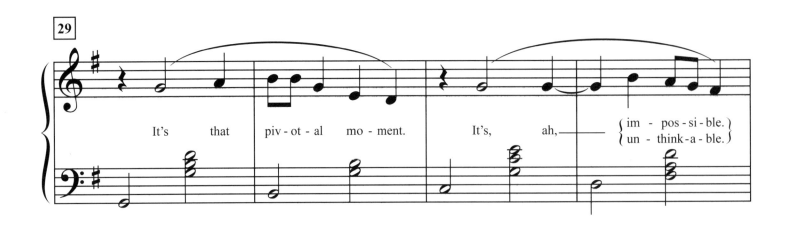

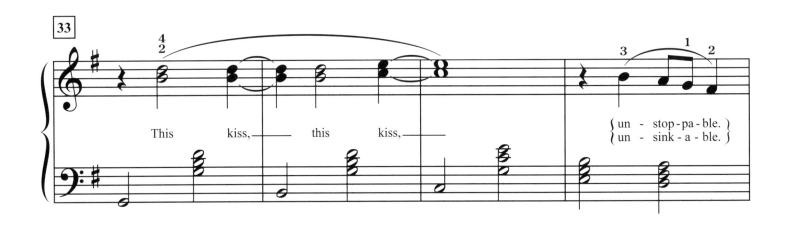

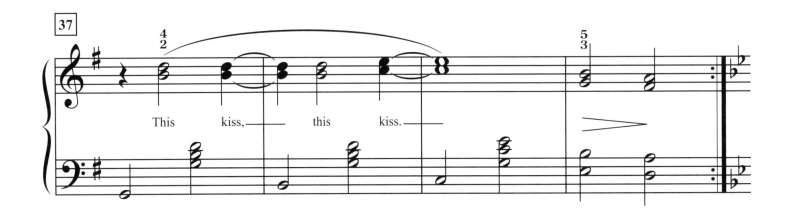

sky,————— oh. You can kiss me with the win - dows o - pen while the

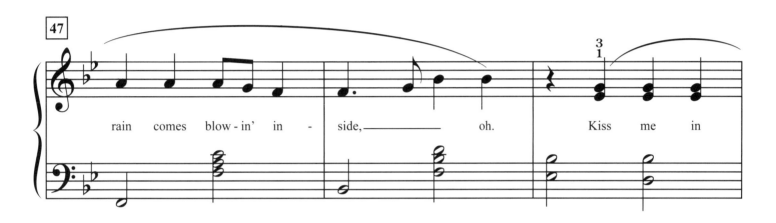

rain comes blow-in' in - side,————— oh. Kiss me in

sweet, slow mo - tion. Let's let ev - 'ry-thing slide.—————

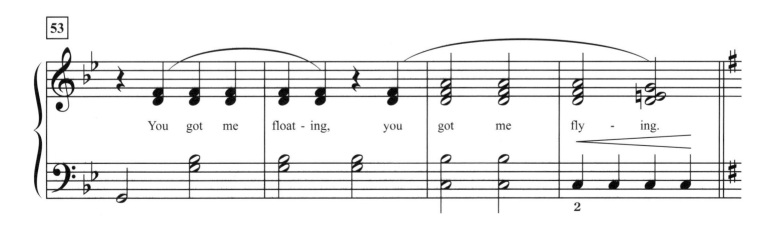

You got me float - ing, you got me fly - ing.

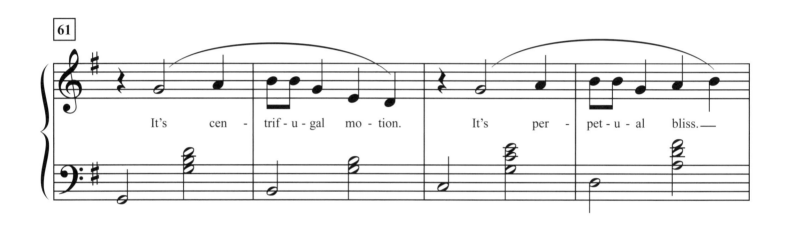

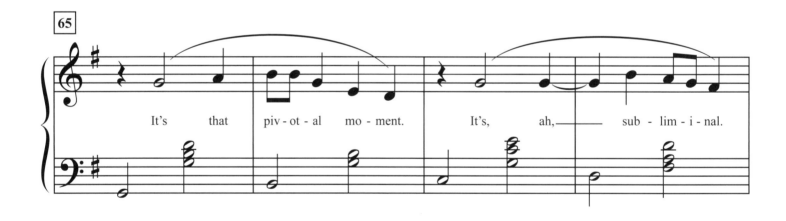

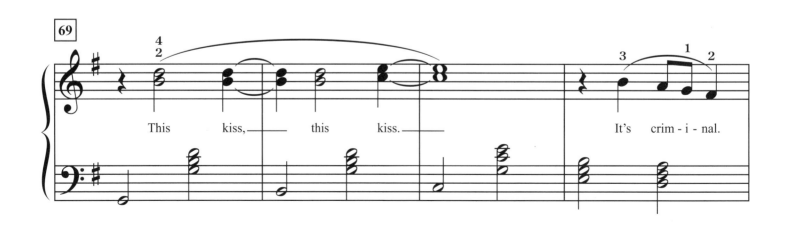

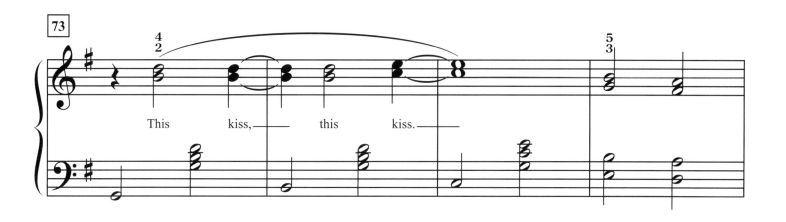

This kiss, this kiss.

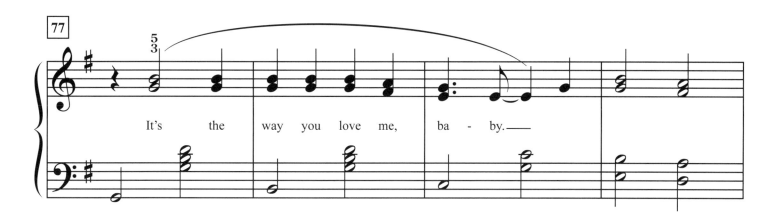

It's the way you love me, ba - by.

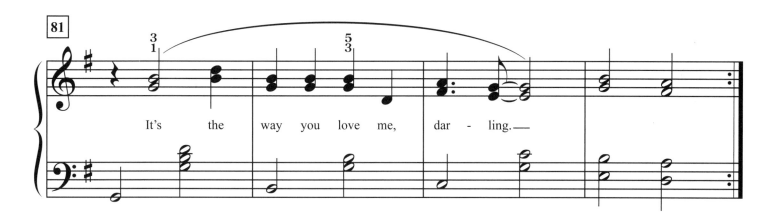

It's the way you love me, dar - ling.

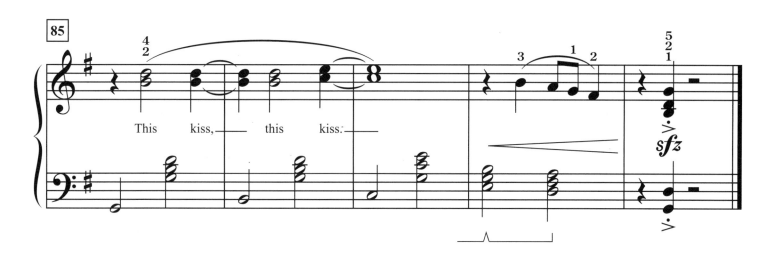

This kiss, this kiss.